Co-Pastor Dachka Brown

718 607-7409

dchKbrown @ yahoo.com

MOTHER'S PRAYER SCEPTRE

MOTHER'S PRAYER SCEPTRE

21 Day Prayer, Fasting and Devotional
Book for Parents with Children
Returning Back to School

Dachka Brown, M.S. Ed.

Library of Congress Control Number: 2015904403
ISBN: Hardcover   978-1-5035-5550-1
                Softcover   978-1-5035-5551-8
                eBook   978-1-5035-5552-5

Scripture quotations marked KJV are from the Holy Bible, King James Version (Authorized Version). First published in 1611. Quoted from the KJV Classic Reference Bible, Copyright © 1983 by the Zondervan Corporation.

Any people depicted in stock imagery provided by Thinkstock are models, and such images are being used for illustrative purposes only. Certain stock imagery © Thinkstock.

Print information available on the last page.

Rev. date: 03/26/2015

To order additional copies of this book, contact:
Xlibris
1-888-795-4274
www.Xlibris.com
Orders@Xlibris.com
708189

CONTENTS

The day was Friday, January 28, 2005, when I gave birth to an eight-pound, seven-ounce baby girl. Our firstborn baby girl, Ayanna, came into this world with a thundering cry at 7:14 p.m. Life brought an entire new meaning. When the nurse placed her in my arms, nothing at that time mattered other than the baby I was holding. Thousands of thoughts began flooding across my mind: *What if I fail miserably at being a mother? Maybe my husband and I should have saved a little bit more money prior to starting a family.* The list goes on and on. At that moment, all I could do was shut my eyes and say aloud these two words to God in prayer, "thank you." Those two simple words, "thank you," have been my initial memoir of a lifelong prayer journey as a mother of now four children.

Prayer is the ultimate source that is essential in our everyday life. Regardless if you're a father, sister, brother, cousin, etc., the need to pray cultivates your life to search deeper within to speak and communicate with our heavenly *Father*. In the Bible, Jesus knew the importance of prayer that *He* taught his disciples how to pray in Luke 11:1–4. After this manner, therefore, pray ye: Our Father which art in heaven, hallowed be thy name. Thy kingdom come. Thy will be done in earth, as it is in heaven. Give us this day our daily bread. And forgive us our debts, as we forgive our debtors.

And lead us not into temptation, but deliver us from evil, for thine is the kingdom and the power, and the glory, forever. Amen.

The need for a prayer and fasting twenty-one-day devotional book is not a cliché or a catchy step by step process for you to read and enjoy, but it's a book where we come together to combat the forces of darkness in high places on behalf of the need of the children. The devil has been lurking at our children's whereabouts and seeking to destroy their future. "Be sober, be vigilant; because your adversary the devil, as a roaring lion, walketh about, seeking whom he may devour" (1 Peter 5:8). "For the weapons of our warfare are not carnal, but mighty through God to the pulling down of strongholds; Casting down imaginations, and every high thing that exalteth itself against the knowledge of God, and bringing into captivity every thought to the obedience of Christ; and having in a readiness to revenge all disobedience, when your obedience is fulfilled" (2 Corinthians 10:4–6).

This is not a parenting book of any sort. However, the focus is geared on praying for our children regardless of how old they may be, as well as a devotional book for you to use on a day-to-day basis. *Devotion* is defined as prayers or religious observance.

As women, God has placed the royal scepter on our tongues to speak life to those things in our children's lives that would direct them and refute those things, which will hinder their growth. The need for discernment is crucial in recognizing those things that will come near their way. "Death and life are in the power of the tongue; and they that love it shall eat the fruit thereof" (Proverbs 18:21).

Scepter is defined as an ornamented staff carried by rulers on ceremonial occasions as a symbol of sovereignty (rod or staff), in which a king, queen, shepherd are symbols of authority. We are placed to have dominion as parents to cover our offspring.

"I will stand upon my watch, and set me upon the tower, and will watch to see what he will say unto me, and what I shall answer when I am reproved. And the LORD answered me, and said, Write the vision, and make it plain upon tables, that he may run that readeth it. For the vision is yet for an appointed time, but at the end it shall speak, and not lie; though it tarry, wait for it, because it will surely come, it will not tarry" (Habakkuk 2:1–3, KJV).

Prayer is defined as one who prays and supplicates. It is the act of addressing supplication to a divinity, especially to the true God, the offering of adoration, confession, supplication, and thanksgiving to the Supreme Being, as public prayer, secret prayer. It is the form of words used in praying, a formula of supplication, an expressed petition, especially a supplication addressed to God, as written or extemporaneous prayer, to repeat one's prayers (www.webster-dictionary.net, 1913 online Webster's Dictionary).

The ability to tap into the heart of God and to sense the channels of where God is taking you in prayer is essential. In prayer, it's not us as mothers in control but God using us as a mouthpiece. Prayer is the compass that directs our path in life.

This book was purposely designed in such a way that finding the availability to pray should not be a concern. It's not so much the quantity but the quality. There is a proverbial phrase that states, "Less is more," by Robert Browning in the nineteenth century. The fervent need to tune out a small portion of your time to pray on behalf of your loved one is the best investment you could ever do.

As you embark on this devotional prayer and fasting book for the next twenty-one days, here are a few questions and answers that will help you along the journey:

Question: Is this book restricted only to mothers?

Answer: No! This book is in no way restricted to just mothers. It's for anyone who has a passion to see children walk in their divine purpose into adulthood.

Question: When should I begin this twenty-one-day devotional prayer and fasting book?

Answer: There is no right or wrong time to begin this twenty-one-day devotional prayer and fasting book. However, I encourage that you set apart allocated time throughout your busy schedule. If you have more time in the morning, then use that time of the day.

Question: Should prayer and fasting be done simultaneously?

Answer: It's strongly encouraged that it be done simultaneously. "Is not this the fast that I have chosen? to loose the bands of wickedness, to undo the heavy burdens, and to let the oppressed go free, and that ye break every yoke?" (Isaiah 58:6). Nevertheless, due to situations that you may not have control of (medical conditions, time restraints at work, nursing [breast-feeding], pregnancy), fasting should not be your number one priority.

Questions: What is fasting?

Answer: Fasting is primarily an act of willing abstinence or reduction from certain or all food, drink, or both, for a period of time.

Under no circumstances should an individual be on an *absolute fast*. Absolute fast is abstinence from all food and liquid for a defined period, usually a single day (twenty-four hours) or several days. Throughout these twenty-one days of fasting, please refrain from an absolute fast or seek your primary physician's advice.

Questions: Can I start this twenty-one-day journey with others?

Answer: Having the support of others in small and large groups, spouse, women groups, book clubs and/or individually is essential to your journey. The need to share your day-to-day personal journey will be encouraging when the dialogue is made between you and others. Yet you may be the only one led in your prayer group to go on this twenty-one-day journey on behalf of your children or youth group.

In the third year of Cyrus king of Persia a thing was revealed unto Daniel, whose name was called Belteshazzar; and the thing was true but the time appointed was long; and he understood the thing, and had understanding of the vision. In those days I was mourning three full weeks. I ate no pleasant bread, neither came flesh nor wine in my mouth, neither did I anoint myself at all, till three whole weeks was fulfilled. And in the four and twentieth day of the first month, as I was by the side of the great river, which is Hiddekel; Then I lifted up mine eyes, and looked, and behold a certain man clothed in linen, whose loins were girded with fine gold of Uphaz: His body also was like the beryl, and his face as the appearance of lightning, and his eyes as lamps of fire, and his arms and his feet like in color to polished brass, and the voice of a multitude. And I Daniel alone saw that vision; for the men that were with me saw not the vision; but a great quaking fell upon them, so that they fled to hide themselves. Therefore I was left alone, and saw this great vision, and there remained no strength in me; for my comeliness was turned in me into corruption, and I retained no strength. Yet heard I the voice of his words and when I heard the voice of his words, then was I in a deep sleep on my face, and me face toward the ground. And, behold, a hand touched me, which set me upon my knees and upon the palms of my hands. And he said unto me, O Daniel, a man greatly beloved, understanding the words that I speak unto thee am I now sent. And when he had spoken these words unto me, I stood trembling. Then said he unto me, Fear not, Daniel: for from the first day that thou didst set thine heart to understand, and to chasten thyself before thy God, thy words were heard, and I am come for thy words. But the prince of the kingdom of Persia withstood me one and twenty days: but, lo, Michael, one of the chief princes, came to help me; and I remained there with the kings of Persia. Now I come to make thee understand what shall befall thy people in the latter days; for yet the vision is for many days. (Daniel 10:1–14)

In the same way, Daniel was attacked and placed in a position where he felt weak and alone. You may find weakness and constraint in many ways. Don't panic! You are heading in the right direction.

Giving No Room for the Devil . . .

Mothers of school-age children. Unlike most fasts done in the past, it's best that you begin on the first day of your child's academic school year/calendar. For example, if your child's first day of school begins on August 9 or September 9, your fast should begin on that day and end twenty-one days later. If you have children who have different first-day dates, then begin on the first day of their academic school month. Example: Child A – August 9; Child B – August 17, then begin your fast on August 1 or August 9.

College/university young adults. Mothers are encouraged to begin fasting on the day their child heads back to college/university.

Early childhood / day care. Mothers are encouraged to begin the first day of class at the center.

Mothers-to-be. Mothers-to-be are encouraged to solely participate in the prayer, not the fasting portion. Your duty is to nurture your unborn baby in his/her fullness.

Women who plan to be mothers in the future. Women who have a great desire to be mothers in the future are strongly encouraged to join in the devotional part of prayer.

Day 1: Commitment/Vow

Hannah

And she vowed a vow, and said, O Lord of hosts, if thou wilt indeed look on the affliction of thine handmaid, and remember me, and not forget thine handmaid, but wilt give unto thine handmaid a man child, then I will give him unto the Lord all the days of his life, and there shall no razor come upon his head. (1 Samuel 1:11)

In the same way, Hannah continued asking God on her behalf for a son. The Lord will prepare you with the tenacity to continue pressing forward toward those things that you want to see happen in your child's life. Hannah was placed in a situation where she was tired of feeling less than a woman in the midst of her rival, Peninnah. There are times when you must tune out everyone around you and set time for fasting and prayer. You must open your mouth and not be afraid of what people may think of you. There are feelings that God have placed in your life to fast on behalf of your child. You may even be ridiculed or looked down by others because people may say that the step you started today is not necessary and try to detour you from the choice you made. *Keep your vow!*

Prayer
Vows

Dear God,

Here I am, Lord! I come before You with my hands lifted up toward heaven. Lord, as Samuel was dedicated to You at a very tender age by the vow his mother, Hannah, stated to *You* ... so am I, right now, giving my child back to You, Lord. Lord, I know that You have great things in store for him/her/them. In spite of what the world says, I believe that You are more than able to break the ruins of the devil and set a clear path for Your child's future. Regardless of the negativity that may come around them this year, I speak life, hope, and peace in their going out and in their coming in. Lord, I pray that they will know Your voice and in the midst of every situation they face. In Jesus's name, I pray. Amen!

Dear God,

Today is my first day of these twenty-one days of fasting for my child(ren), (state your child's name) _____. Father, I come to You humbly at Your feet, knowing that I make this commitment to You to let my ways become Your ways in this fast. Lord, I come to You as a mother (grandmother, aunt, sister, guardian, niece, neighbor, teacher, etc.) with my heart and mind focused on You in regard to the needs of this new academic school year/ year. I give this child back to You, and, Lord, may *Your* will be made perfect in his/her life. Lord, as Samuel was dedicated to You at a tender age, I commit everything concerning my unborn baby, infant, toddler, school-age child, preteen, teenager, young adult to You once again.

Day 1 Reflections

Day 2: Wisdom

Abigail

But one of the young men told Abigail, Nabal's wife, saying, Behold, David sent messengers out of the wilderness to salute our master; and he railed on them. But the men were very good unto us, and we were not hurt, neither missed we any thing, as long as we were conversant with them, when we were in the fields. They were a wall unto us both by night and day, all the wilt we were with them keeping the sheep. Now therefore know and consider what thou wilt do; for evil is determined against our master, and against all his household: for he is such a son of Belial, that a man cannot speak to him. Then Abigail made haste, and took two hundred loaves, and two bottles of wine, and five sheep ready dressed, and five measures of parched corn, and an hundred clusters of raisins, and two hundred cakes of figs, and laid them on asses. And she said unto her servants, Go on before me; behold, I come after you. But she told not her husband Nabal. (1 Samuel 25:14–19)

As easy as it may seem to others, we know that not one child is alike. Think of two parents who have twins; regardless if they're identical or fraternal, they are unique and have their own characteristics. We must respect our children's individual creativity and ways of learning. *Wisdom* is defined as the ability to think and act using knowledge, experience, understanding, common sense, and insight. The need to set appropriate goals for our children is needed for them to reach their highest potential, even if they are faced with emotional and physical challenges.

Prayer

Dear God,

You, and You alone, know my heart and can lead my heart toward the direction You want my child(ren) to go. Without Your wisdom guiding them/him/her, where will they be? Lord, I ask You to increase their/his/her wisdom this academic school year from making sudden decisions on their/his/her own without first considering You. The need to be able to communicate with others around them today is what will help them in the future. Let them follow Your words and Your road map, which is in Your word daily. Just as Abigail was able to make a good judgment at a time when her family's life depended on it, so I am asking You, heavenly Father, to sharpen those necessary tools of wisdom, knowledge, and understanding, O God. Lord, let me not be confused at the time of decision making, but allow me to see through Your lenses. You have placed us on this earth to have dominion. For Your word declares in 1 Timothy 6:17, "Charge them that are rich in this world, that they be not highminded, nor trust in uncertain riches, but in the Living God, who giveth us richly all things to enjoys; that they do good, that they be rich in good foundation against the time to come, that they may lay hold on eternal life." The life we demonstrate daily around others is truly what we sow in our future. The need to not be so focused on our own needs but to see the needs of others will, in return, be a blessing to others as well. There will be opportunities that will come in their lives, but grant them the wisdom to choose wisely in what's best. Amen.

Day 2

Day 3: Patience

Anna, the Prophetess

And there was one Anna, a prophetess, the daughter of Phanuel, of the tribe of Aser: she was of great age, and had lived with an husband seven years from her virginity; And she was a widow of about fourscore and four years, which departed not from the temple, but served God with fasting and prayer night and day. And she coming in that instant gave thanks likewise unto the Lord, and spake of him to all them looked for redemption in Jerusalem. And when they had performed all things according to the law of the Lord, they returned into Galilee, to their own city Nazareth. And the child grew, and waxed strong in spirit, filled with wisdom: and the grace of God was upon him. Now his parents went to Jerusalem every year at the feast of the Passover. (Luke 2:36–41)

Dear God,

I stretch my hands to heaven and ask for patience in my child's life. Though circumstances around them/him/her may appear to be in small pieces and difficult for them to put all together, I pray that Your arms would cover them and grant them clarity from those things in their lives that seem to take a long time to occur. Move away those things that easily come and distract them from waiting on Your season in life. Amen.

We may say that Anna didn't have a care in the world since she spent most of her entire life living in the temple praying. She was waiting for the manifestation of our Lord and Savior, Jesus Christ, to one day walk into the temple. It was then after seeing Jesus that she was enlightened and saw the promise come to life. "But they that wait upon the Lord shall renew their strength, they shall mount up with wings as eagles, they shall run and not be weary and they shall walk, and not faint" (Isaiah 40:31, KJV). Anna's patience was exercised daily when she held on to the word that *Jesus* was going to be born, to redeem a nation.

Journal 3

Day 4: Leadership

Deborah

And the children of Israel again did evil in the sight of the Lord, when Ehud was dead. And the LORD, sold them into the hand of Jabin king of Canaan, that reigned in Hazor; the captain of whose host was Sisera, which dwelt in Harosheth of the Gentiles. And they children of Israel cried unto the LORD: for he had nine hundred chariots of iron; and twenty years he mightily oppressed the children of Israel. And Deborah, a prophetess, the wife of Lapidoth, she judged Israel at that time. And she dwelt under the palm tree of Deborah between Ramah and Bethel in mount Ephrahim; and the children of Israel came up to her for judgment. (Judges 4:1–5)

Dear God,

I come to You today on behalf of (state the child[ren]'s name) at this moment. Father, I know that there is greatness inside of them, and I ask that You build those qualities of leadership within them/him/her. Lord, don't let them go unnoticed by their teachers, coaches, peers, and social environment. The need to procrastinate will no longer take residence in their lives. They will desire to remain focused and be godly leaders who represent

You in their daily character. I counteract and forfeit any spirit of depression and low self-esteem right now. Amen.

Firstly, I want to applaud every single parent raising his/her children without or with minimal support from their children's father/mother. The need to solely provide for a child can be challenging in so many ways, yet the benefits are rewarding. Just like Deborah who stood in the gap when there was no one suitable at the time to lead Israel, it is a pivotal time for us now and then to see how God can use a challenging situation to something magnificent. "Can a woman forget her sucking child, that she should not have compassion on the son of her womb? Yea, they may forget, yet will I not forget thee" (Isaiah 49:15, KJV).

It's difficult for a mother to watch her child who is helpless and in need of essential things. That child may feel incompetent if she is not able to provide. It was never God's intent for a woman to raise children by herself. Yet sometimes, life brings unexpected surprises that leave us in a place when we must advocate for our child's well-being, especially if you're juggling, working full-time, attending school, or taking care of a sick family member in your care. Being a single parent should never be taken lightly but taken with a devoted prayer life and benefits from our mind, soul, and spirit. That's why it's essential that the center of focus is on praying to our Lord and Savior, Jesus Christ.

The prophetess was able to lead because she was able to hear from God. She aimed her leadership on hearing from God on what to do. When we pray, we must be able to pray with a focus on what we want to see occur. "Ye ask, and receive not, because ye ask amiss, that ye may consume it upon your lusts" (James 4:3). The word "amiss" means inappropriate or not quite right and out of line or place. We should always have our minds in tune to what God is directing us to pray for.

Journal 4

Day 5: Help/Endurance

Rizpah

But the king took two sons of Rizpah the daughter of Aiah, whom she bare unto Saul, and Armoni and Mephibosheth; and the five sons of Michal the daughter of Saul, whom she brought up for Adriel the son of Barzillai the Meholathite: And he delivered them into the hands of the Gibeonites, and they hanged them in the hill before the LORD: and they fell all seven together, and were put to death in the days of harvest, in the first days, in the beginning of barley harvest. And Rizpah the daughter of Aiah took sackcloth, and spread it for her upon them out of heaven, and suffered neither the birds of the air to rest on them by day, nor the beasts of the field by night. And it was told David what Rizpah the daughter of Aiah, the concubine of Saul, had done. And David went and took the bones of Saul and the bones of Jonathan his son from the men of Jabesh-gilead, which had stolen them from the street of Beth-shan, where the Philistines had hanged them, when the Philistines had hanged them, when the Philistines had slain Saul in Gilboa. And he brought up from thence the bones of Saul and the bones of Jonathan his son; and they gathered the bone of them that was hanged. And the bones of Saul and Jonathan his son buried they in Zelah, in the sepulchre of Kish his father; and they performed all that the king commanded. And after that God was intreated with the land. (2 Samuel 21:8–14)

Dear God,

I stand here in need of my child(ren)'s safety this academic school year. Lord, direct them/him/her each and every day as they walk, drive, ride on the school bus to their various schools, day care, after-school activities, playground, work, etc. Lord, be their eyes, ears, nose, feet, and hands when they're weak. Send the spiritual alarm right now to confuse the very plans of the devil. Any demon that sits high and lurks to detour them, I command you to take flight right now. Let no weapon that is formed against them prosper. I come against every contrary situation that will bring fear or intimidation to their well-being. I rebuke every spirit of accidents and incidents that come to forfeit the plans You have in their/his/her life. Remove every mishap in my child's life that he/she may be against from the legal aspect that may want to occur or have occurred. I take a stand.

Journal 5

Day 6: Courage

Esther

Now it came to pass on the third day, that Esther put on her royal apparel, and stood in the inner court of the king's house, over against the king's house, and the kind sat upon his royal throne in the royal house, over against the gate of the house. And it was so, when the king saw Esther the queen standing in the court, that she obtained favour in his sight; and the king held the sceptre that was in his hand, So Esther drew near, and touched the top of the sceptre. Then said the king unto her, What wilt thou, queen Esther? And what is thy request? It shall be even given thee to the half of the kingdom. And Esther answered. If it seem good unto the king, let the king and Haman come this day unto the banquet that I have prepared for him. Then the king said, Cause Haman to make haste, that he may do as Esther hath said. So the king and Haman came to the banquet that I Esther had prepared. And the king said unto Esther at the banquet of wine, What is thy petition? And it shall be granted thee; and what is thy request? Even to the half of the kingdom it shall be performed. Then answered Esther, and said, My petition and my request is: If I have found favor in the sight of the king, and if it pleases the king to grant my petition and to perform my request, let the king and Haman come to the banquet that I shall prepare for them, and I will do tomorrow as the king hath said. (Esther 5:1–8)

Dear God,

I send forth Your spirit of courage to reign in and through their lives, the courage to set a stand to maintain a firm declaration to stand for righteousness. Lord, the ability to know the truth and not be ashamed to let others know or see the path they have willingly taken. Lord, we know that fear is cancerous and has the ability to spread in their thoughts and prohibit them from pursuing the dreams You have set for them. Anoint them with the spirit of Joshua to be courageous even in the time of uncertainties or when the ways look dim. In spite of their failures in the past, let them have the desire to get up and do it again. Allow them to pursue the path by being steadfast on the promises that You have created for them. The need for them to put their trust in you, even when it may seem that no one is willing to step forward in their personal biblical faith.

Journal 6

_____

_____

_____

_____

_____

_____

_____

_____

_____

_____

_____

_____

_____

_____

_____

_____

_____

_____

_____

_____

_____

_____

_____

_____

_____

_____

_____

_____

_____

Day 7: Dedication

Mary and Martha

Now it came to pass, as they went, that he entered into a certain village: and a certain woman named Martha received him into her house. And she had a sister called Mary, which also sat at Jesus' feet, and heard his word. But Martha was cumbered about much serving, and came to him, and said, Lord, dost thou not care that my sister hath left me to serve alone? Bid her therefore that she help me. And Jesus answered and said unto her, Martha, Martha, thou are careful and troubled about many things: But one thing is needful: and Mary hath chosen that good part, which shall not be taken away from her. (Luke 10:38–42)

Dear God,

I come before Your throne, knowing that You are able to do exactly what You promised. In spite of their busy schedule, I ask that they would set time apart for You daily by attending a local college chapel, church, devotion, and prayer time at home (younger children). I pray that You will remain as the center of their attention as they pursue academic success. Lord, allow them to know how to balance their time with schoolwork and time for You. Set the atmosphere where they will be able to build their prayer and devotional time with You. It is You, God, that has kept them thus far, and it is You that will continue walking with them. Furthermore, grant them the ability to be balanced in setting time aside just for You. Amen.

Journal 7

_____
_____
_____
_____
_____
_____
_____
_____
_____
_____
_____
_____
_____
_____
_____
_____
_____
_____
_____
_____
_____
_____
_____
_____
_____
_____
_____
_____
_____
_____

Day 8: Friendship

Ruth

And Naomi said, Turn again, my daughters: why will ye go with me? Are there yet any more sons in my womb, that thou may be your husbands? Turn again, my daughters, go your way; for I am too old to have a husband. If I should say, I have an husband also to night, and should also bear sons; Would you tarry for them till they were grown? Would you stay for having husbands? Nay, my daughters; for it grieveth me much for your sakes that the hand of the LORD is gone out against me. And they lifted up their voices and wept again: and Orpah kissed her mother in law; but Ruth clave unto her. And she said, Behold, thy sister in law; but Ruth clave unto her. And she said, Behold, they sister in law is gone back into her people, and unto her gods: return thou after thy sister in law. And Ruth said, intreat me not to leave thee, or to return from following after thee: for whither thou goest, I will go; and where thou lodgest, I will lodge, thy people shall be my people and they God my God: Where thou diest, will I die, and there will I be buried: the LORD do so to me, and more also if ought but death part thee and me. When she saw that she was steadfastly minded to go with her, then she left speaking unto her. (Ruth 1:12–18)

Dear God,

This day, I set my face toward *You* in need of uniting them/him/her with productive friendships. I pray, O God, that You will tear down every friendship that will bring abuse, low self-esteem, bullying, verbal and nonverbal abuse around or to them. Set an atmosphere where they will grow as a tender plant amid a place that may seem lonely and unfriendly. I remove every target or negative enforcer that will easily remove them from feeling the warmth of meeting people who share similar goals in life and are able to stand firm on the word of God concerning the promises You decreed over them. Give them the need to build friendships that are not predicated on what they/he/she do or does but on the ways that are pleasing toward God—a God-fearing friendship that is encouraging and enlightening in the path of God. Amen.

Journal 8

Day 9: Guilt

Sarah

Now Sarai Abram's wife bare him no children: and she had an handmaid, an Egyptian, whose name was Hagar. And Sarai said unto Abram, Behold now, the LORD hath restrained me from bearing; I pray thee, go in unto my maid; it may be that I may obtain children by her. And Abram hearkened to the voice of Sarai. And Sarai Abram's wife took Hagar her maid the Egyptian, after Abram had dwelt ten years in the land of Canaan, and gave her to her husband Abram to be his wife. And he went in unto Hagar, and she conceived: and when she saw that she had conceived, her mistress was despised in her eyes. And Sarai said unto Abram, My wrong be upon thee: I have given my maid into the bosom; and when she saw that she had conceived, I was despised in her eyes: the Lord judge between me and thee. (Genesis 16:1–5)

Dear God,

I remove the spirit of guilt that comes over my child(ren) that prohibits them from going forward academically, spiritually, emotionally, socially, etc. I command that the mistakes of yesterday will not distract them from their tomorrow. I ask You,

Lord, to instruct them on how to deal with matters that may arise in their lives. Jeremiah 6:16 says, "Thus saith the LORD, stand ye in the paths, where is the good way, and walk therein, and ye shall find rest for your souls. But they said, We will not walk therein." To let go of hurt, shame, and mishaps in life, one needs to first realize that the only one that is hurting is you. Moving on in life and the need to put aside the thoughts that always arise in our mind can be quite difficult if you don't totally surrender the situation 100 percent to God. In life, we tend to just give You what we want in our life and hold back those things concerning our life that are hard to let go. Lord, You are ready for me to give You my personal life—growing up when I was violated, taken advantage, indulged in behaviors that made me hate myself. The need to know that I placed my situation at Your feet is the best choice I ever made for me and my entire family.

Amen.

Journal 9

Day 10: Wholeness

Syrophoenician Woman

For a certain woman, whose young daughter had an unclean spirit, heard of him, and came and fell at his feet: The woman was a Greek, a Syrophoenician by nation; and she besought him that he would cast forth the devil out of her daughter. But Jesus said unto her, Let the children first be filled: for it is not meet to take the children's bread, and to cast it unto the dogs. And she answered and said unto him, Yes, Lord: yet the dogs under the table eat of the children's crumbs. And he said unto her, For this saying go thy way; the devil is gone out of thy daughter. And when she was come to her house, she found the devil gone out, and her daughter laid upon the bed. (Mark 7:25–30)

Dear God,

Father, I come before You as a servant—a servant who is seeking more of You and less of me. The need to get lost in Your presence is the place where I see myself in You, O God. Lord, my desire is to be at the place where I have access to You no matter what others may say. Though I sometimes deem myself unworthy to even bow in Your presence with all my shortcomings, I know You are more than able to meet my every need. The need for You to see about my need is urgent, and I've cried too long about the same thing. "Hear my cry, O God attend unto my prayer. From the end of the earth will I cry unto thee, when my heart is overwhelmed: lead me to the rock that is higher than I. For thou hast been a shelter for me, and a strong tower from the enemy. I will abide in thy tabernacle for ever: I will trust in the covert of thy wings" (Psalm 61:1–4, KJV). Lord, if You don't step in and take control of my situation, I will just lose it. So, Lord, right now, I need You to make my health, family, finances, job, _____ _____whole. I need to walk in the fullness and in the promises that You have promised me.

Journal 10

_____
_____
_____
_____
_____
_____
_____
_____
_____
_____
_____
_____
_____
_____
_____
_____
_____
_____
_____
_____
_____
_____
_____
_____
_____
_____

Day 11: Perseverance

Shunammite Woman

And when the child was grown, it fell on a day, that he went out to his father to the reapers. And he said unto his father, my head, my head. And he said to a lad, Carry him to his mother. And when he had taken him, and brought him to his mother, he sat on her knees till noon, and then died. And she went up, and laid him on the bed of the man of God, and shut the door upon him, and went out. And she called unto her husband, and said, Send me, I pray thee, one of the young men, and one of the assess, that I may run to the man of God, and come again. And he said, Wherefore wilt thou go to him to day? It is neither new moon, nor Sabbath. And she said, it shall be well. Then she saddled an ass, and said to her servant, Drive and go forward; slack not thy riding for me, except I bid thee. So she went and came unto the man of God to mount Carmel. And it came to pass, when the man of God saw her afar off, that he said to Gehazi his servant, Behold, yonder is that Shunammite. Run now, I pray thee, to meet her and say unto her, Is it well with thee? Is it well with thy husband? Is it well with the child? And she answered, it is well: And when she came to the man of God to the hill, she caught him by the feet: but Gehazi came near to thrust her away. And the man of God said, Let her alone; for her soul is vexed within her: and the Lord hath hid it from me, and hath not told me. Then she said, Did I desire a son of my lord? did I not say, Do not deceive me? Then he said to Gehazi, Gird up thy loins, and take my staff in thine hand, and go thy way: if thou meet any man, salute him not; and if any salute thee, answer him not again; and lay my staff upon the face of the child. And the mother of the child said, As the LORD liveth, and as thy souls liveth, I will not leave thee. And he arose, and followed her. And Gehazi passed on before them, and laid the staff upon the face of the child; but there was neither voice, nor hearing. Wherefore he went again to meet him and told him saying, The child is not awaked. And when Elisha was come into the house, behold, the child was dead, and lay upon his bed. He went in therefore, and shut the door upon them twain, and prayed unto the LORD. And he went up, and lay upon the child, and put his mouth upon his mouth, and his eyes upon his eyes, and his hands upon his hands: and stretched himself upon the child; and the flesh of the child waxed warm. Then he returned, and walked in the house to and fro; and went up, and stretched himself upon him, and the child sneezed seven times, and the child opened his eyes. And he called Gehazi, and said, Call this Shunammite. So he called her. And when she was come in unto him, he said, Take up thy son. Then she went it, and fell at his feet, and bowed herself to the ground, and took up her son, and went out. (2 Kings 4:18–37)

Dear God,

You said that the race is not given to the swift or the strong but to those who endure till the end (Ecclesiastes 9:11). I come to You at this hour, asking for perseverance for my child(ren) to continue running this race with patience. Lord, I ask that they will continue everything that they put their mind to do for the growth and development of their success. Grant them a steadfast mind and heart to pursue those things, just as the Shunammite didn't slack her riding in the need of her dead son. So I'm right now coming to You on a matter that You have promised me concerning my children. As difficult as things may appear to be, I know that the end of a matter is better than its beginning. Patience of spirit is better than haughtiness of spirit (Ecclesiastes 7:8, KJV). My child's aspiration in life may appear dead to his/her teachers, coach, employer, and family members, but I know what You decreed and declared in their lives. I am convinced that in spite of our present situation, our destiny is not predicated on what people around me say or do. "I will worship toward thy holy temple, and praise thy name for thy lovingkindness and for thy truth; for thou hast magnified thy word above thy name" (Psalm 138:2). You have placed Your word before Your name—so, God, what You decreed and declared, I know You will allow me to accomplish.

Journal 11

_____

_____

_____

_____

_____

_____

_____

_____

_____

_____

_____

_____

_____

_____

_____

_____

_____

_____

_____

_____

_____

_____

_____

_____

_____

_____

_____

_____

_____

Day 12: Timing

Jephthah's Daughter

And Jephthah vowed a vow unto the LORD, and said, If thou shalt without fail deliver the children of Ammon into mine hands, Then it shall be, that whatsoever cometh forth of the doors of my house to meet me, when I return in peace from the children of Ammon, shall surely be the LORD'S, and I will offer it up for a burnt offering. So Jephthah passed over unto the children of Ammon to fight against them; and the LORD delivered them into his hands. Then it shall be that whatsoever cometh forth of the doors of my house to meet me, when I return in peace from the children of Ammon, Shall surely be the LORD'S, and I will offer it up for a burnt offering. So Jephthah passed over unto the children of Ammon to fight against them; and the LORD delivered them into his hands. And he smote them form Aroer, even till thou come to Minnith, even twenty cities, and unto the plain of the vineyards, with a very great slaughter. Thus the children of Ammon were subdued before the children of Israel. And Jephthah came to Mipeh unto his house, and, behold, his daughter came out to meet him with timbrels and with dances: and she was his only child; beside her he had neither son nor daughter. And it came to pass, when he saw her, that re rent his clothes, and said, Alas my daughter! Thou has brought me very low; and thou are one of them that trouble me; for I have opened my mouth unto the LORD, and I cannot go back. And she said unto him, My father, if thou hast opened thy mouth unto the LORD, do to me according to that which hath proceeded out of thy mouth; forasmuch as the LORD hath taken vengeance for thee of thine enemies, even of the children of Ammon. And she said unto her father, Let this thing be don for m; let me alone two months, that I may go up and down upon the mountains, as bewail my virginity, I and my fellows. And he said, Go. And he sent her away for two months: and she went with her companions, and bewailed her virginity upon the mountains. And it came to pass at the end of two months, that she returned unto her father, who did with her according to his vow which he had vowed: and she knew no man. And it was a custom in Israel, That the daughters of Israel went yearly to lament the daughter of Jephthah the Gileadite four days in a year. (Judges 11:30–40)

Dear God,

I send Your angels right now to go into time and capture those moments that are needed for our children to succeed. Lord, I ask that You set Your angels to take charge of their going out and their coming in. They may be young and frail to understand what tomorrow holds for them, but with the grace of God, I know that You will allow them to grow to be men and women of tomorrow. Lord, just as You extended fifteen more years to King Hezekiah in 2 Kings 20:6, "And I will add unto thy days fifteen years; and I will deliver thee and this city out of the hand of the king of Assyria; and I will defend this city for my own sake; and for my servant David's sake."

Journal 12

Day 13: Health

The Woman with the Issue of Blood

And a woman having an issue of blood twelve years, which had spent all her living upon physicians, neither could be healed of any, Came behind him, and touched the border of his garment: and immediately her issue of blood stranched. And Jesus said, Who touch me? When all denied, Peter and they that were with him said, Master, the multitude throng thee and press thee, and sayest thou, Who touched me? And Jesus said, Somebody hath touched me: for I perceive that virtue is gone out of me. And when the woman saw that she was not hid, she came trembling, and falling down before him, she declared unto him before all the people for what cause she had touched him, and how she was healed immediately. And he said unto her, Daughter, be of good comfort: thy faith hath made thee whole; go in peace. (Luke 8:43–48)

Dear God,

I dismiss any physical or emotional illness that may seek to overtake our children in their lives. I cast out every demonic spirit that lingers and festers in their mind, class, room, home, and studies. Grant them the ability to give You those stains that are difficult to remove, for Your blood will remove every stain. I counteract right now every plan that their enemy has placed over their eyes to blind them so that they can't see their purpose in life. Lord, touching and reaching Your scepter will pierce the enemy's heel and stop him from trespassing into godly territory in Jesus's name.

Amen.

Journal 13

Day 14: Hope

Mary

And in the sixth month the angel Gabriel was sent from God unto a city of Gabriel was sent from God unto a city of Galilee, named Nazareth, To a virgin espoused to a man whose name was Joseph, of the house of David; and the virgin's name was Mary. And the angel came in unto her, and said, Hail, thou that art highly favoured, the Lord is with thee: blessed art thou among women. And when she saw him, she was troubled at his saying, and cast in her mind what manner of salutation this should be. And the angel said unto her, Fear not, Mary: for thou hast found favor with God. And, behold, thou shalt conceive in the womb, and bring forth a son, and shalt call his name JESUS. He shall be great, and shall be called the son of the Highest: and the Lord God shall give unto him the throne of his father David: And he shall reign over the house of Jacob for ever, and of his kingdom there shall be no end. Then said Mary unto the angel, How shall this be, seeing I know not a man? And the angel answered and said unto her, The Holy Ghost shall come upon thee, and the power of the Highest shall overshadow thee: therefore also that holy thing which shall be born of thee shall be called the Son of God. And, behold, thy cousin Elisabeth, she hath also conceived a son in her old age: and this is the sixth month with her, who was called barren. For with God nothing shall be impossible. And Mary said, Behold the handmaid of the Lord; be it unto me according to thy word. And the angel departed from her. (Luke 1:26–38)

Dear God,

Heavenly Father, I send forth Your word right now in their present situation. Lord, uphold their ways and keep them from falling and grant them hope for the days ahead in life. Your word in Jeremiah 33:3 states that we call unto You, and You will show us things that we have not known or seen yet. Keep their hearts leaping with great expectation. Amen.

Journal 14

Day 15: Salvation

The Samaritan Woman

And he must needs go through Samaria. Then cometh he to a city of Samaria, which is called Sychar, near to the parcel of ground that Jacob gave to his son Joseph. Now Jacob's well was there. Jesus therefore, being wearied with his journey, sat thus on the well: and it was about the sixth hour. There cometh a woman of Samaria to draw water: Jesus saith unto her, Give me to drink. For his disciples were gone away unto her, Give me to drink. For his disciples were gone away unto the city to buy meat. Then saith the woman of Samaria unto him, How is that thou, being a Jew, askest drink of me, which am a woman of Samaria? For the Jews have no dealings with the Samaritans. Jesus answered and said unto her, if thou knewest the gift of God, and who it is that saith to thee, Give me to drink; thou wouldest have asked of him, and he would have asked of him, and he would have given thee living water. The woman saith unto him, Sir, thou hast nothing to draw with, and the well is deep: from whence then hast thou that living water? Art thou greater than our father Jacob, which gave us the well, and drank thereof himself, and his children, and his cattle? Jesus answered and said unto her, Whosoever drinketh of this water shall thirst again: But whosoever drinketh of the water that I shall give him shall never thirst; but the water that I shall give him shall be in him a well of water springing up into the everlasting life. The woman saith unto him Sir, give me this water, that I thirst not, neither come hither to draw. Jesus saith unto her, Go, call thy husband, and come hither. The woman answered and said, I have no husband. Jesus said unto her, Thou hast well said, I have no husband: For thou hast had five husbands; and he whom thou now hast is not thy husband: in that sadist thou truly. The woman saith unto him, Sir, I perceive that thou art a prophet. Our fathers worshipped in this mountain; and ye say, that in Jerusalem is the place where men ought to worship. Jesus said unto her, Woman, believe me, the hour cometh, when ye shall neither in this mountain, nor yet at Jerusalem, worship the Father. Ye worship ye know not what: we know what we worship: for salvation is of the Jews. But the hour cometh, and now is, when the true worshippers shall worship the Father in spirit and in truth: for the Father seeketh such to worship him. God is a Spirit: and they that worship him must worship him must worship him in spirit and in truth. The woman saith unto him, I know that Messias cometh, which is called Christ: when he is come, he will tell us all things. Jesus saith unto her, I that speak unto thee am he. And upon this came his disciples, and marveled that he talked with the woman; yet no man said, What seeketh thou? or, Why walketh thou with her? The woman then left her waterpot, and went her way into the city, and saith to the men, Come, see a man, which told me all things that ever I did: is not this the Christ? Then they went out of the city, and came unto him. (John 4:4–30)

Dear God,

I come before You not just for my child but also on behalf of my friends' child(ren)'s salvation right now. Romans 10:9–10 states "that if thou shalt confess with thy mouth the Lord JESUS, and shalt believe in thine heart that God hath raised him from the dead, thou shalt be saved. For with the heart man believeth unto righteousness; and with the mouth confession is made unto salvation." Lord, Your desire is that no one perishes but has life more abundantly. Amen.

Journal 15

Day 16: Finances

The Widow's Oil

Now there cried a certain woman of the wives of the sons of the prophets unto Elisha, saying. Thy servant my husband is dead; and thou knowest that thy servant did fear the LORD: and the creditor is come to take unto him my two sons to the bondmen. And Elisha said unto her, What shall I do for thee? Tell me, what hast thou in the house? And she said, Thine handmaid hath not any thing in the house, save a pot of oil. Then he said, Go, borrow thee vessels abroad of all thy neighbors, even empty vessels; borrow not a few. And when thou art come in, thou shalt shut the door upon thee and upon thy sons, and shalt pour out into all those vessels, and thou upon thy sons, and shalt pour out into all those vessels, and thou shalt set aside that which is full. So she went from him, and shut the door upon her sons, who brought the vessels to her; and she poured out. And it came to pass, when the vessels were full, that she said unto her son, Bring me yet the vessel. And he said unto her, There is not a vessel more. And he said, Go, sell the oil and pay thy debt, and lie thou and thy children of the rest. (2 Kings 4:1–7)

Dear God,

My need today is that You will open the door of finances to complete the tasks that You have placed in front of them. Lord, Your desire is for us to be good stewards over our increase. Your word declares the earth is for the Lord and the fullness thereof. So whatever You have created at our reach, our thoughts and prayers are to obtain those things. Just like the workers whom You granted the talents to bring back their wages, we must not neglect that You require the same for us as believers—the need to walk in total obedience by following Your word by tithing and giving You the first fruit of our harvest.

Journal 16

Day 17: Resources

Lydia

And a certain woman named Lydia, a seller of purple, of the city of Thyatira, which worshipped God, heard us: whose heart the Lord opened, that she attended unto the things which were spoken of Paul. And when she was baptized, and her household, she besought us, saying, if you have judged me to be faithful to the Lord, come into my house, and abide there. And she constrained us. (Acts 16:14–15)

Dear God,

I pray for You to open the windows of opportunities in this academic school year. Lord, I ask that You grant them favor in receiving financial funds (scholarships, grants, tuition payments) to be granted for the furtherance of their higher education. I dismiss the atmosphere of lack that will prevent them from pursuing the plan in their lives. The spirit of success will overshadow them continually in their going out and going in. *"The LORD shall command the blessing upon thee in thy storehouses, and in all that thou settest thine hand unto; and He shall bless thee in the Land which the LORD thy God giveth thee"* (Deuteronomy 28:8). Lord, You are *El Shaddai (Hebrew word),* "*the All-sufficient One" or "the God who is more than enough,"* and everything I know You will provide.

Journal 17

Day 18: Relentless

Rebekah

And Isaac was forty years old when he took Rebekah to wife, the daughter of Bethuel the Syrian of Padanaram, the sister to Laban the Syrian. And Isaac intreated the LORD for his wife, because she was barren: and the LORD was intreated of him, and Rebekah his wife conceived. And the children struggled together within her; and she said, If it be so, why am I thus? And she went to inquire of the LORD. And the LORD said unto her, two nations are in thy womb, and two manner of people shall be separated from thy bowels; and the one people shall be stronger than the other people; and the elder shall serve the younger. And when her days to be delivered were fulfilled, behold, there were twins in her womb. (Genesis 25:20–24)

Prayer

Dear God,

I come behalf every unborn dream, vision and aspiration that has not been birthed yet. I ask oh God that you will grant us with the need to seek you even for my friends, family members who may be struggling with infertility and having difficulty with having children of their own. Lord, let them find confidence in

You as they not watch the tides the rises but on your word that you pronounced in their life. I curse every doubt that may arise in their circumstances. Lord, we know it not our will but thine will be done. Lord, as Rebekah/Women we know we are carrying a weight of responsibilities in our life. The need to carry the promise in our womb is also needed for us to spiritually sense what God is going to do in our womb in the future. The need to inquire daily on the behalf of my children even before they are born is granting me access to destroy the plans of the devil. We hold our standards of the Blood stain of Jesus high so the devil is well aware that we are aware of his devises in JESUS NAME

Journal 18

Day 19: Advocate/Spokesperson

Nathan and Bathsheba

Wherefore Nathan spake upon Bathsheba the mother of Solomon, saying, Hast thou not heard that Adonijah the son of Haggith doth reign, and David our lord knoweth it not? Now therefore come, let me, I pray thee, give thee counsel, that thou mayest save thine own life, and the life of thy son Solomon. Go and get thee in unto king David, and say unto him, Didst not thou, my lord, O king, swear unto thine handmaid, saying, Assuredly, Solomon thy son shall reign after me, and he shall sit upon my throne? Why then doth Adonijah reign? Behold, while thou yet talkest there with the king, I also will come in after thee, and confirm thy words.

And Bathsheba went in unto the king into the chamber: and the king was very old; and Abishag the Shunammite ministered unto the king. And Bathsheba bowed, and did obeisance unto the king. And the king said, What wouldest thou? And she said unto him, My lord, thou swarest by the LORD thy God unto thine handmaid, saying, Assuredly Solomon thy son shall reign after me, and he shall sit upon my throne. And now, behold, Adonijah reigneth; and now, my lord the king, thou knowest it not: And he hath slain oxen and fat cattle and sheep in abundance, and hath called all the sons of the king, and Abiathar the priest and Joab the captain of the host: but Solomon thy servant hath he not called. And thou, my lord, O king, the eyes of all Israel are upon thee, that thou shouldest tell them who shall sit on the throne of my lord the king after him. Otherwise it shall come to pass, when my lord the king shall sleep with his fathers, that I and my son Solomon shall be counted offenders. And, lo, while she yet talked with the king, Nathan the prophet came in. And they told the king, saying, Behold Nathan the prophet. And when he was come in before the king, he bowed himself before the king with his face to the ground. And Nathan said, My lord, O king, has thou said, Adonijah shall reign after me, and he shall sit upon my throne? (1 Kings 1:11–24)

Dear God,

I stand in proxy right now for every child who is in need of a source of covering and protection. Your word declares that you have given us the power to pull down every strong hold and movement that may arise in their lives. Lord, as children they may not be able to defend themselves so Lord we stand in the gap of intercessory prayer. Your word declares whatever we bind on earth shall be bound in heaven: and whatever you shall loose on earth shall be loosed in heaven. Matthew 16:19 My cry is that you would send your angels to protect their gates as they go out and come in. I remove every violating spirit that may lurk around them in secret. We take charge right now with the power of the holy ghost that is within us to be dismissed right now in the mighty name of JESUS NAME.

Journal 19

Day 20: Creativity

Eve

And Adam gave names to all cattle, and to the fowl of the air, and to every beast of the field; but for Adam there was not found an help meet for him. And the LORD God caused a deep sleep to fall upon Adam, and he slept: and he took one of his ribs, and closed up the flesh instead thereof; And the rib, which the LORD God had taken from man, made he a woman, and brought her unto the man. And Adam said, This is now bone of my bones, and flesh of my flesh: she shall be called Woman, because she was taken out of Man. (Genesis 2:20–23)

Dear God,

Father, I come to You right now with my heart centered on You, for You are a Sovereign God that made the heaven and the earth. I bow before Your presence for Your awesomeness. I give my heart, mind, soul, and spirit to You. Lord, I come to You today on behalf of my children. You know those talents within them that You have given the day before they were conceived in the womb. Lord, I ask that You would mold and shape their creativity to the perfection of Your will. Sharpen their minds, O God, to utilize their talents (arts, music, acting, sports, etc.). I rebuke the spirit of inadequacy that prohibits them from seeking new opportunities and goals in life. Jeremiah 29:11–12 declares, "For I know the thoughts that I think toward you, saith the Lord, thoughts of peace, and not of evil, to give you an expected end. Then shall ye call upon me, and ye shall go and pray unto me, and I will hearken unto you." Allow them not to bury their talents prematurely but give them a tenacious spirit that rises above every obstacle in Jesus's name. Amen.

Journal 20

_____
_____
_____
_____
_____
_____
_____
_____
_____
_____
_____
_____
_____
_____
_____
_____
_____
_____
_____
_____
_____
_____
_____
_____
_____
_____
_____
_____

Day 21: Virtuous Woman

Who can find a virtuous woman? For her help is far above rubies. The heart of her husband doth safely trust in her, so that he shall have no need of spoil. She will do him good and not evil all the days of her life. She seeketh wool, and flax, and worketh willingly with her hands. She is like the merchants' ships; she bringeth her food from afar. She riseth also while it is yet night, and giveth meat to her household, and a portion to her maidens. She considereth a field, and buyeth it: with the fruit of her hands she planteth a vineyard. She girdeth her loins with strength, and strengtheneth her arms. She perceiveth that her merchandise is good: her candle goeth not out by night. She layeth her hands to the spindle, and her hands hold the distaff. She stretcheth out her hand to the poor, yea she reacheth forth her hands to the needy. She is not afraid of the snow for her household: for all her household are clothed with scarlet. She maketh herself coverings of tapestry; her clothing is silk and purple. Her husband is known in the gates, when he sitteth among the elders of the land. She maketh fine linen, and selleth it; and delivereth girdles unto the merchant. Strength and honour are her clothing and she shall rejoice in time to come. She openeth her mouth with wisdom; and in her tongue is the law of kindness. Her children arise up, and call her blessed; her husband also, and he praiseth her. Many daughters have done virtuously, but thou excellest them all.

Favor is deceitful, and beauty is vain; but a woman that feareth the LORD, she shall be praised. Give her of the fruit of her hands; and her own works praise her in the gates. (Proverbs 31:10–31)

Dear God,

My heart is fixed on You! I know that Your word is the same yesterday, today, and forever; and Your promises are sure in my families, youth group, students, children, grandchildren, etc., in life throughout their going out and their coming in. Deuteronomy 28:1–3 declares that *"We shalt hearken diligently unto the voice of the LORD thy God, to observe and to do all his commandments which I command thee this day, that the LORD thy God will set thee on high above all nations of the earth. And all these blessings shall come on thee, and overtake thee, it thou shalt hearken unto the voice of the LORD thy God. Blessed shalt thou be in the city, and blessed shalt thou be in the field."*

This generation would not die spiritually and physically to the devices of the enemy. You have given us the tool, which is prayer and fasting, to break every chain that the enemy has placed over our young people. They will be assets to our society; they will become the head and not the tail. I cast away every sudden fear and place boldness right now in Jesus's name. Amen.

Journal 21

_____
_____
_____
_____
_____
_____
_____
_____
_____
_____
_____
_____
_____
_____
_____
_____
_____
_____
_____
_____
_____
_____
_____
_____
_____
_____
_____
_____
_____

The heart of every parent is to see their child (children) walk in the perfect will of God. The perfect will of God should not be confused with our personal will for our children. It is but God's divine will in our children's life.

Lo, children are an heritage of the Lord: and the fruit of the womb of his reward. As arrows are in the hand of a mighty man; so are children of the youth. Happy is the man that hath his quiver full of them: they shall not be ashamed, but they shall speak with the enemies in the gate. (Psalm 127:3–5)

As parents, guardians, grandparents, youth leaders, etc., we are at a place where we must not compromise or substitute God's word over our own. The focus should be centered on having God's will done in their lives.

I will stand upon my watch, and set me upon the tower, and will watch to see what he will say unto me, and what I shall answer when I am reproved. And the LORD, answered me, and said, Write the vision, and make it plain upon tables, that he may run the readeth it. For the vision is yet for an appointed time, but at the end it shall speak, and not lie; though is tarry, wait for it; because it will surely come, it will not tarry. (Habakkuk 2:1–3)

The need to build a prayer life is the key to be able to pull down those strongholds in our families' curses in the past that may appear in our children and their future.

For the weapons of our warfare are not carnal, but mighty through God to the pulling down of strong holds. (2 Corinthians 10:4)

God has given us the authority to pull down every strong mind, soul, and spirit.

In the beginning of each academic school year, the name of Jesus should resound not just in our children's ear but for every student, administrator, janitor, school safety, school aid, school nurse, guidance counselor, transportation services, food worker should be covered under the blood of *Jesus*.

The Bible states in Proverbs 18:21, "*Death and life are in the power of the tongue: and they that love it shall eat the fruit thereof.*" As adults, we must be mindful in removing any negative verbal usage or words that will allow our children to feel less of themselves. As we may already know, what we say can tamper or build them; however, we must be honest with our children when they have a need to be corrected. This can also foster self-fulfilling prophecy.

A self-fulfilling prophecy is a prediction that directly or indirectly causes itself to become true, by the very terms of the prophecy itself, due to positive feedback between belief and behavior. (wikipedia.org)

Printed in the United States
By Bookmasters